David Paige
**Behind the Scenes
at the Zoo**
Photographs Roger Ruhlin

Albert Whitman & Company, Chicago

Library of Congress Cataloging in Publication Data

Paige, David.
    Behind the scenes at the zoo.

    SUMMARY: Text and photographs present the special
work of establishing and maintaining a zoo.
    1.   Zoological gardens—Juvenile literature.
[1.   Zoological gardens]   I.   Ruhlin, Roger.   II.   Title.
QL76.P3   590'.744   77-22214
ISBN 0-8075-0613-3

Acknowledgments

This book is dedicated to all those people who work behind the scenes to accomplish the true purpose of a zoo: to provide an important facility for nature appreciation, education, conservation, research, and recreation.

■

The author and photographer wish to thank the many persons who cooperated in the preparation of this book. Their special appreciation goes to the Director, Dr. Lester E. Fisher, and the Assistant Director, Dennis A. Meritt, Jr., and the Staff of Lincoln Park Zoo, Chicago; to the Director and Staff of the San Diego Zoo and the San Diego Wild Animal Park; and to Lion Country Safari, Inc., Laguna Hills, California.

Contents

∎

Animals for the Zoo

■

Think of zoos, and you immediately think of animals, from antelopes to zebras, from tiny lizards to tall giraffes. How does a zoo acquire these animals? It's all part of what goes on behind the scenes at the zoo.

The 500-pound baby and the zoo director

Not many people fly across an ocean in a huge jet, bottle-feeding a baby elephant every two hours during the flight. But that is what Dr. Lester Fisher, director of the Lincoln Park Zoo of Chicago, did. And he was performing one of the many activities that go on behind the scenes at a zoo.

This story began in a dense jungle in Asia, months before Dr. Fisher's flight.

A baby elephant was found wandering alone on Sri Lanka, an Asian island near the equator, just off the tip of southern India. No one knew what had happened to the baby's mother, but she had disappeared. The little elephant, weak and hungry, was too young to survive long by itself.

You may ask what on earth anyone would do who found a weak, hungry, orphaned baby elephant.

On Sri Lanka, there is an answer. The baby is taken to an elephant orphanage. There, the staff cares for it until a suitable, permanent home is found.

Officials at the zoo in Chicago learned that a baby Asiatic elephant was available for adoption. It was an animal they wanted for their zoo, one which they needed. As a healthy adult, this elephant could be used for breeding, to mate with another Asiatic elephant and

◄
This llama at the San Diego Zoo seems to invite you to step behind the scenes for a glimpse of what goes on at a zoo.

have young born at the zoo. This was important because Asiatic elephants were on the list of endangered species.

You may know that certain kinds, or species, of animals are so rare that the species is in danger of disappearing entirely if planning is not done to save it. Breeding such animals as the Asiatic elephant at the zoo may keep the endangered species from dying off.

Many arrangements had to be made for the adoption of the baby elephant. Application forms were filled out by members of the Chicago zoo staff and sent to the wildlife authorities in Sri Lanka. Money had to be found for the cost of the elephant and its transportation. Proper permits had to be obtained from the governments of Sri Lanka and the United States.

Bozi, the baby Asiatic elephant orphaned in Sri Lanka, gulps milk from a bottle held by Dr. Lester E. Fisher, director of Lincoln Park Zoo in Chicago.

Days went by, and at last information came to the zoo that the baby elephant was ready to travel—*if* someone from the zoo could supervise the trip.

So it was that Dr. Fisher traveled halfway around the world to a tropical island in the Indian Ocean to take charge of this valuable animal. He had to make sure its journey would be safe and comfortable.

Up and away!

When everything was in order in Sri Lanka, the elephant was put into a roomy, sturdy crate. Even though it was still a baby, the elephant weighed 500 pounds, more than most full-grown lions and three times as much as Dr. Fisher.

The elephant traveled in the cargo section of the plane. Dr. Fisher sat in the passenger cabin. But every two hours during the entire 24-hour flight, he left his seat to go to the cargo section.

Like babies of many species, the little elephant could drink milk from a bottle. But unlike most baby mammals, this one eagerly drank two gallons of milk at a feeding. Being a baby-sitter for an elephant on a long trip was no easy matter!

In Chicago, a crowd waited at the airport to greet the zoo's newest arrival.

Officials from the United States Customs Bureau and the U.S. Fish and Wildlife Service were there to make

This full-grown Asiatic elephant at the San Diego Zoo is about nine feet from shoulder to ground and weighs about four tons. A female, she has no tusks.

sure all rules were obeyed in bringing this animal into the country. There were also representatives from the airline company and the airport, as well as members of the zoo staff.

Permits, health certificates, and other necessary papers were all carefully checked and approved. Not until then was the newcomer officially accepted. From the airport, it was only a short ride by truck to the zoo and a new home for this Asiatic elephant.

What animals for which zoo?

Obtaining the animals a zoo displays is a behind-the-scenes activity which involves the skill and know-how of many people.

No matter how big it is, a zoo must make choices. The San Diego Zoo, with the largest collection in the world, has more than 5,000 animals, representing some 1600 species and subspecies. But this is only a sample of the more than one million species of animals known to exist.

A zoo in a large city may have 2,000 to 3,000 animals from perhaps 500 species and subspecies. A collection might include animals as different as a king cobra and a kangaroo, a grizzly bear and a vampire bat, or even an orangutan and a pangolin. A small zoo may house as many as a thousand animals, although of course not a thousand separate species.

If every zoo had the same selection of animals, it would be dull indeed. To avoid this, zoos tend to specialize in some particular way. One zoo may emphasize the wildlife of its own region. Another may strengthen its collection of great apes, but offer only a few other primates.

A zoo must keep the right number of animals for its needs and at the same

The pangolin is also called a scaly anteater. It is about three feet long, and like some armadillos, it can curl itself into a ball if attacked. Pangolins are found in southeastern Asia and in Africa, south of the Sahara Desert.

time provide an interesting variety. It will constantly add, replace, trade, and sell animals to keep the zoo population at the right level.

For Sale: 1 Siberian Tiger

How an animal will be obtained often depends upon what it is. Some are easy to find and ship; others, like the baby elephant from Sri Lanka, require special care. But one thing is sure: it is easier today to populate a zoo than it was in the mid-1800s when the first zoos in the United States were being set up.

In the past, staff members of a zoo were often involved in the actual capture of animals to be exhibited. To the jungles of Africa, Asia, and South America, to the frozen lands of the Arctic, to forests, mountains, and deserts, there zoo people went.

These expeditions frequently involved scientific observation and the discovery of new facts about animals and their environment. Such expeditions were costly and time-consuming, and sometimes dangerous as well.

Today, by comparison, the task of stocking a zoo seems easy. In fact, the most common method of acquiring animals is simply to buy from or trade with another zoo. If the zoo in Atlanta, Georgia, has an extra timber wolf, it may want to trade the wolf to the San Diego Zoo for a Grant's gazelle. Or, if New

York's Bronx Zoo suddenly finds itself with a new litter of cheetahs, several may be sold to collections seeking such animals.

All the zoo staff has to do is check the want ads—a rather special set of want ads, it's true. They appear in the American Association of Zoo Parks and Aquariums Newsletter. There are ads from zoos throughout the United States, much like the one here.

PHILADELPHIA ZOOLOGICAL GARDEN
Philadelphia, Pennsylvania 19104
Contact: Curators
SURPLUS

Males/Females

1/0 Lowland Gorilla,	$8,000
app. 7 years	or breeding loan
1/1 Siberian Tiger	2,000
0/1 Black Leopard,	
b.7-8-60	2,750
0/1 Indo-Chinese Leopard,	
b.7-8-68	750
1/0 Puma, adult breeder	175
0/1 Guanaco, b.6-17-73	250
5/0 African Dwarf Goat	each 40
	or group 175
0/1 Black Swan	150
3/4 New Zealand Scaup	pair 120
5/7 Lesser Brazilian Teal	pair 100
3/1 Cape Teal	
(2 males, $65 each)	pair 150

WANTED

0/1 Dik-Dik	0/1 Ratel
0/1 Eland	0/1 Cape Hyrax
0/2 Barasingha	0/1 Baird's Tapir
0/1 Margay	

11

What animal is being shipped out? Each crate contains a wild sheep, or mouflon.

The price of a zoo animal depends upon many things, including age, condition, and scarcity. Just as prices in stores rise and fall as times change, so also do animal prices.

If a zoo cannot get what it needs from another zoo, there are wild animal dealers who will acquire the animal. In a way, these dealers take the place of the zoo staff of long ago who went out to bring back particular wild animals.

If an animal dealer cannot obtain the animal ordered by trade or purchase, he will ask professional hunters to go out and capture it.

By plane, ship, or truck to a zoo home

Locating the animal the zoo wants is only the first step. Getting the animal to the zoo is the next. Dr. Fisher's baby Asiatic elephant had its own physical requirements. There were also special conditions set by the government of Sri Lanka.

Each animal, large or small, has its own needs to be met. Certainly a rhinoc-

This baby gorilla, born in the wild in West Africa, was flown to Chicago in 1963. As an adult, she has twice become a mother at Lincoln Park Zoo.

Chicago Park District Photo

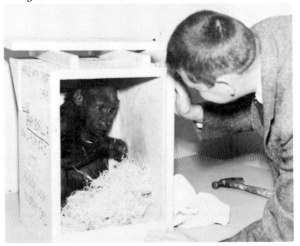

eros cannot be shipped in the way that a porpoise travels.

Animals which must be transported over long distances are usually sent by air because it is the fastest method of travel.

For short journeys on land, trucks are commonly used.

No matter how it travels, the animal must be crated, caged, or glass-enclosed, according to its needs. During the time it will travel the animal must have food and water, strict temperature control, safety and comfort. If necessary, someone may travel with the animal to look after its welfare. There must be clear instructions for handling. The safety of anyone—an airline employee, for example—who might have contact with the animal must be considered.

If the animal is entering the United States from another country, it is normally quarantined on its arrival. This means that it is kept away from other animals for a period of time, for there is always the chance that an animal may bring disease organisms or parasites with it.

The U.S. government has set up well-equipped centers where an animal can be kept in isolation (that is, by itself), usually for about 30 days. At the center, the animal is checked for disease and its general health is thoroughly examined.

Born at the zoo

Zoo staffs add to their collections by trading animals with other zoos. They

Transporting an adult black rhinoceros, an animal on the endangered species list, is no easy task.

add a few animals obtained through professional dealers. But more and more, most collections depend upon animals which have been born right at the zoo.

Suppose the lions brought from an Asian jungle grow old and in time die. Their place is taken by lions who were cubs born in the same zoo.

Today, many species of animals, from polar bears to garter snakes, mate and reproduce in captivity.

A large zoo may have as many as 500 or even a thousand individual newborn mammals, birds, and reptiles in a single year.

The San Diego Wild Animal Park, the largest of its kind in the United States, recorded the birth of 78 different species of animals in a recent year.

Breeding, then, is important because it enables the zoo to maintain its own population and to produce animals for other zoos. All this means that zoos of today are much less dependent than they were in the past on taking animals out of their original homes, which may be distant or otherwise difficult to reach.

Breeding programs are valuable in another way. They let zoologists, the scientists who study animals, observe them from birth onward. Such close observation may be almost impossible in the wild.

Jim Klepitsch for the Chicago Sun-Times

Miki-Luk (Eskimo for "Little One") was three months old when she was photographed. Rejected by her polar bear mother, she was hand-raised by Kevin Bell, a curator at Lincoln Park Zoo. She was kept in the Bird House to protect her from diseases mammals might have.

Zoos to the rescue

A special benefit of breeding has already been mentioned. For endangered species, healthy breeding in a zoo can make the difference between survival and disappearance.

Recently there were only 200 known Indian lions alive anywhere in the world. Of these, a male and female at Lincoln Park Zoo, in Chicago, produced ten offspring. This meant that there was a five per cent increase in the Indian lion population of the world, and it took place at just one zoo.

The entire population of the Hawaiian goose, the state bird of Hawaii, was almost destroyed by hunters and dogs. By 1950, only 30 birds could be found. How these birds were saved is a good example of the international coopera-tion that goes on behind the scenes at many zoos.

Three of the Hawaiian geese were shipped to a bird sanctuary in England, in the hope they could be bred there. About 15 years later, 100 young birds were ready to return to Hawaii. Today, the Hawaiian goose, known there as nene (pronounced nay-nay), is no longer an endangered species.

The cheetah, an endangered species, is being bred in substantial numbers at the San Diego Wild Animal Park, where this photograph was taken.

Hazards zoo babies encounter

Not too long ago, breeding at the zoo was rarely successful. Now it is much more common, but it is still not easy.

Zoo conditions must be set up to encourage animals to mate. Then care must be taken before and after the young are born.

An animal mother must have special care and attention during gestation, the period of pregnancy. She must have a place where birth can take place safely. A bear may withdraw to a den, for example, and not exhibit her cubs until some time after birth. A mother giraffe needs a straw-covered floor so that her baby will not be injured by dropping at birth on hard concrete.

Once the baby is born, it, too, must be watched carefully. Like human beings, animals can be good parents, not-so-good parents, or even dangerous parents. In fact, some animals, most reptiles, for example, do not take care of their young. Zoo workers must provide care and protection whenever necessary.

Male animals will sometimes kill or menace their young offspring. They cannot be allowed in the same area with mothers and babies. And of course an infant animal can be hurt by a mishap or by its mother's clumsiness. Sometimes, a baby is rejected by its mother. Then quick action must be taken to remove

The mother giraffe appears to be standing guard over her baby, one of many zoo-born animals.

the little one to safety and give it a chance to survive.

For many reasons an animal may spend its early days in the zoo infirmary or nursery until it is able to live on its own. A baby mammal is sometimes placed in the same kind of crib used for newborn human babies who need special care. There it is protected against infection and fed at the right intervals.

Gifts and givers

There is still another way that zoo collections are enlarged. This is by donation.

Unusual animals have often been prized gifts, the kind an explorer might send to a royal patron, or one government give to another as a sign of friendship.

The government of China in 1972 presented two very rare giant pandas to the United States. This gift was meant to show an interest in opening friendly relationships between the two big nations. The pandas attracted many visitors to the National Zoological Park in Washington, D.C., where they were exhibited.

An individual zoo may be singled out for a gift from abroad. The Bronx Zoo, the familiar name for the New York Zoological Park, was once given three African elephants, together weighing three tons. There was a requirement,

however: as in the more recent case of the baby elephant from Sri Lanka, these elephants had to be escorted by members of the zoo staff to their new home. Supervising and shipping those special charges proved a challenge.

In England, a zoo director received a telephone call from a man who said he had an Indian cobra that he would like to give to the zoo. The director did not

These rare and endangered Indian lion cubs are bottle-fed at Lincoln Park Zoo by a volunteer. Both cubs want attention at once.

believe him. What, after all, would an ordinary citizen be doing with one of the world's most poisonous snakes?

The director politely said that the zoo would gladly accept the cobra—if indeed the man had one to donate. Then he waited.

Several days later, the man appeared, carrying a large, flimsy cardboard box. The whole thing was a joke, just as he suspected, the zoo director thought. No one would carry a cobra in a box like that.

The director took the box and lifted the lid. A large, very real cobra reared up and spread its hood in anger. The zoo director slammed the lid closed. He decided quickly that the man was not joking.

Luckily, very few people have cobras they want to give away. It is far commoner for zookeepers to be offered pet alligators, small wild birds, or turtles. Not many of these gifts fit into a big collection, and most must be refused or another home found for them.

The mother zebra nuzzles her newborn baby, born at the San Diego Zoo.

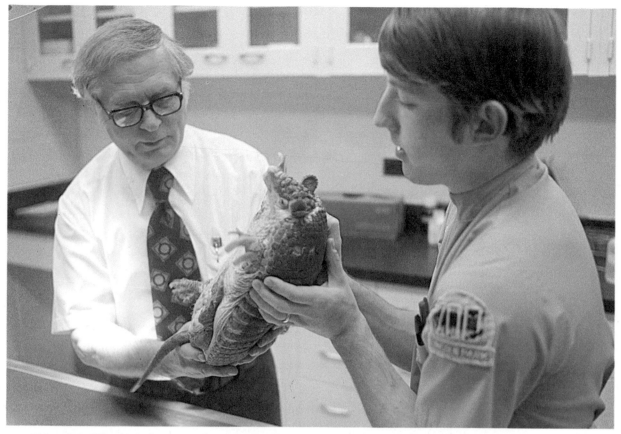

This armadillo is being examined in the infirmary by Dr. Erich R. Maschgan, Lincoln Park Zoo veterinarian.

The new animal enters its zoo home

Everything that keeps an animal alive and well in a zoo depends on human beings.

An armadillo, looking much like a miniature armored dinosaur, is ready to be added to the zoo's collection. It will be entirely dependent on the care humans give it. Who will these caretakers be?

First, there are the curators, who direct everything which has to do with the animals under their supervision. Curators are usually scientists who have studied biology (the science of living things) and zoology (the branch of biology which deals with animals).

At a small zoo, there may be only one curator. In a large zoo, there generally will be a curator for each class of animals: mammals, birds, reptiles, and fish.

The curator is familiar with the needs of the animals under his or her care. On a regular tour through the zoo, the curator is quick to spot an animal that appears to behave in an unexpected way. Is the animal sick? Has it been hurt? What can be done? These are questions the curator asks and then must answer.

The second person who will be concerned for the new armadillo is an animal keeper. Keepers look after the needs of the animals in their care. They are responsible for feeding, cleaning, and being alert to how the animals behave.

Animal keepers are often men and women who have been interested in animals for as long as they can remember. Some of them have had college courses in biology and zoology. They are almost always people with much practical experience and what is called "animal sense." They know danger signals. They are concerned for each animal's individual needs and personality.

The third person who welcomes the new animal to the zoo is the veterinarian, a doctor who is qualified to take care of animals' health. Size determines whether a zoo will have its own veterinarian or will have to depend upon a veterinarian in the community.

Each chimpanzee wants a share of the carrots and grapes their keeper, Jim Higgins, is offering.

The new armadillo is kept in isolation after its arrival at the zoo. It is put by itself to make sure it is healthy. It may be inoculated against disease and checked to see that it is free of parasites.

At this time the animal is introduced to the diet it will be fed at the zoo. The armadillo will be closely watched to make sure it eats its food and that the food furnishes enough nourishment.

Not everything goes as planned

At times, an animal can baffle its keeper, the veterinarian, and the curator. A 20-foot-long python with the unlikely name of Elsie was one such creature in an English zoo. Elsie refused to eat anything for eight months. Her death seemed sure. Then suddenly Elsie began to eat what the zoo had to offer, and all was well. Some animals, however, have starved to death when the zookeeper, in spite of all effort, has been unable to provide the right food or the appropriate eating conditions.

When everyone responsible for the new animal is convinced the time has come, the next step is taken. The animal joins the zoo family and is introduced to its new environment, or surroundings.

Now, at last, the newcomer is ready to meet the animals with which it will live. There will be other animals nearby as well, and as in a human community, there may be trouble with neighbors.

This small ferret is very much an individual to its keeper, David Kahn. Too thirsty to wait for a drink, it's getting special attention.

Alice, a full-grown, 15-year-old elephant, was brought to the Bronx Zoo. When she was being led to the area where she would live, a lion in a nearby cage suddenly roared. Alice panicked and broke away from the keeper who was leading her. She ran into the reptile house, taking the door and part of the wall with her. Once inside, she would not budge—and it is next to impossible to move a 4,500-pound elephant if she doesn't want to move. Finally her former keeper was called in, and he somehow convinced Alice to walk to her new area. Once there, she adjusted to life at the Bronx Zoo. It was no longer strange because the zoo had become her home.

Building the Zoo

■■

There are hundreds, even thousands, of animals. Each needs its own space, its own needs met. How to solve housing a zoo collection is one of the biggest challenges to be met behind the scenes.

Can an animal be "at home" in a zoo?

In nature, the area where an animal lives is called its habitat. The polar bear's habitat, for example, is the frozen land and sea of the Arctic. A steamy-hot tropical rain forest is the habitat where the big-beaked toucan is at home.

In its natural habitat, an animal finds food, protection from its enemies, a place to have its young, and perhaps shelter from heat or cold, rain or drought. Many living creatures are so specialized that they must have certain features in their habitats. A perching bird is at home in trees; a hippopotamus must have water in which it can bathe, wallow, and play.

An important behind-the-scenes task at a zoo is to recreate the conditions required by a particular animal for healthy survival. An artificial habitat is built to resemble as closely as possible the bird's, reptile's or mammal's natural habitat.

Tigers in the shadow of city buildings

Forests, tall grasslands, and swamps in Asia are habitats of wild tigers. These animals need the protection of shadows, where their striped coats are a good camouflage. Unlike some animals, tigers live in a wide range of climate, from hot and tropical to snowy and frigid.

Tigers are meat-eaters and in their natural habitat often hunt at night. As adults, they live alone, but males will share their territory with one or more females.

A city zoo cannot provide the large area tigers roam in the wild. But the zoo can provide shaded areas, rocks, shrubs, and trees. The tigers can mark these

◄
It's a cold day in Chicago, but the Humboldt penguins and the California sea lions enjoy the winter sunshine.

23

with their own scent to lay claim to a territory. They can sharpen their claws on logs and use a "litter environment" for toilet purposes. A safe sleeping place is also required. If the zoo habitat has these essentials, tigers can lead healthy lives.

How different needs are met

Each habitat at the zoo is scientifically planned by the zoologists and biologists on the staff. The tiger is only one kind of animal in the zoo collection. There are many others, and each has its own spe-cial needs, its own distinct set of conditions necessary for healthy living.

The sea lions, for example, swim in an artificial sea that contains more than 250,000 gallons of water, enough to fill four large swimming pools. Their environment must have islands where the animals can rest and sunbathe. The pool itself requires an elaborate system to filter and recirculate the water to keep it clean. Another system maintains the temperature at a steady level, no matter what the air temperature may be.

Do you think of tigers as jungle animals? They live in a wide range of climates, and snow does not bother these Siberian tigers, a rare and endangered species.

Here's a realistic desert setting for a Western diamondback rattlesnake. It may look as if it's outdoors, but it is behind glass.

One zoo habitat often houses more than a single species of animal. The penguins, for example, can share the same habitat built for the sea lions. Obviously two species that cannot exist peaceably side by side in the wild need different habitat settings. Most of the meat-eating large mammals need a space of their own, away from antelopes and deer or whatever is their natural prey.

In the reptile house there is a wide variety of small habitats and some larger ones as well. The rattlesnake is housed in an enclosure which recreates a desert scene, complete with sand, cactus, rocks, and hot, dry air.

The giant anaconda, a South American snake which sometimes grows to 30 feet in length, requires more space and a setting which mimics a river bank or swamp. There is a pond, with logs and large tree branches, where the snake can climb and curl. The air is warm and humid.

Night into day

Bats and other animals which sleep in the daytime and are active at night pose problems for zookeepers. A sleeping bat or a grasshopper mouse curled into a ball does not make an interesting exhibit during the zoo's daytime hours.

With the help of research, zoos are now able to turn day into night for these nocturnal creatures. Lights almost invisible to the animals let visitors see them awake and busy. At night, other lights duplicate daylight, and the animals sleep.

The mouselike animal from western South America, the degu, is nocturnal. At Lincoln Park Zoo, its days have been changed around so that visitors can see it when it is active.

Uninvited guests

Birds are kept in a number of different environments. Tropical birds are housed in an aviary where the indoor climate, the trees, vines, and flowering plants, create a jungle-like setting.

Other birds live in large outdoor aviaries, sometimes built like huge cages, sometimes like simple enclosures. Some birds, such as peacocks and ducks, cannot or will not fly away. Water birds need ponds for swimming and wading. Perching birds need trees and shrubs, and there must be safe nesting places.

Often the outdoor habitats for birds are so attractive that uninvited feathered visitors fly in—and some stay. Wild birds, like owls, ducks, hawks, and geese, swoop down for free food. Many are soon on their way, but others earn the nickname of moochers. Zoo workers sometimes have to evict them.

These flamingoes have no objections to sharing a pond with gulls and terns.

Planning to meet zoo needs takes the attention of Dr. Fisher, director, and Dennis A. Meritt, Jr., assistant director, at Lincoln Park Zoo.

Zoos change

Animals don't change, but zoos do. Directors and curators and animal specialists look for new ways to house animals and at the same time make zoos fascinating and educational. The planning is a constant behind-the-scenes activity.

Not so long ago, animals stared out through bars as you stared at them. Rows of cages looked like a prison, and very little was done to create environments in which animals could feel and act as if they were at home.

The large outdoor habitat, now a popular part of most zoos, often began with a monkey island. This was usually a miniature rocky mountain surrounded by a wide water-filled moat which kept monkeys and their audience apart.

The monkey island was stocked with monkeys and perhaps mountain goats and bighorn sheep. The monkeys had freedom to climb, chase, play tricks, and hide. They behaved pretty much as monkeys do in the wild, except that they didn't have to search for food.

Next, city zoos found room for outdoor habitats for sea lions, penguins, and even porpoises. Now, even though space may be limited, there are habitats for elephants, hippos, rhinos, giraffes, zebras, the bears, the big cats, and the smaller animals like foxes, jack rabbits, prairie dogs, and ground hogs. If an area is small, it can be improved by adding logs, rocks, and trees. An animal that swings on vines in the jungle finds a swing of heavy rope an acceptable substitute.

Planning comes first

Building an artificial habitat on a large scale is one of the most complex and costly projects a zoo can undertake. Such a habitat may take two years or more in planning and building and cost as much as a million dollars.

First, the zoo staff, the director, curators, and various specialists, hold planning sessions. This is the time to review what is known about the physiology, the

Building a setting like this requires a knowledge of animals and the skills of architects, engineers, and builders who design and complete it. The location is the San Diego Zoo.

This polar bear may seem to be surrounded by ice and snow, but in southern California, that's impossible. The artificial setting does, however, suggest how the bear lives in the Arctic.

habits, and the natural habitat of the animals that are to be exhibited. Polar bears, for instance, live where snow and ice abound, but these are not practical materials for a zoo setting. Substitutes must be used. If the habitat is for tropical animals, then temperature and humidity are important.

Animals in the wild face danger all the time. A lion may leap on a baby giraffe, an owl swoop down on a scampering mouse. A hunter may shoot a leopard for its spotted coat. But the zoo director has no wish to risk the lives of his valuable animals. In planning, safety cannot be forgotten, ever.

Zoo safety concerns the animals, the zoo workers, and of course the public. Some precautions are hidden behind the scenes, as in the case of first-aid supplies which might be needed in an emergency at the reptile house. Locks on doors and cages have to be ones clever apes cannot open.

Many outdoor habitats are separated by a water-filled moat from viewers. A curious child cannot get too close, and the animals on display cannot escape.

Here knowledge of animal behavior is important—a leopard can leap as much as twelve feet. A narrow moat might not be enough of a barrier to insure safety.

Visitors at the zoo can endanger animals. If this is hard to believe, think of the popcorn, candy, papers, sticks, and stones thrown at elephants and bears. Birds are sometimes mischievously attacked. Some infectious human diseases can be caught by animals.

With so much to consider, planning requires time and care.

The builders arrive

Once the experts at the zoo have made their plans, the work of building the habitat is turned over to a team of architects and engineers. They draw up the actual plans for construction. Then the contractors come in to handle the building, buying and installing of plumbing, wiring, and finishing materials.

Mountains are made of concrete or other mixtures sprayed over wire mesh. Corridors and entrances are built, moats dug, walls and barriers constructed, water piped in.

Then the landscapers add their talents. The appropriate trees, shrubs, and plants are put in place. Boulders, logs, and the shoreline of ponds get attention.

When all the work is done, the habitat is inspected and ready for the animals to live in and the animal keepers to maintain. Visitors exclaim, "How natural!"

and few think of the many workers who created a successful artificial habitat.

But does it work?

Even when artificial habitats have been carefully planned, there may be surprises awaiting the zoo people once the animals are moved in.

At one zoo, an orangutan was upset by the white wall in its enclosure. It did not calm down until the wall was painted a cool green.

The fence used to pen in bison was so constructed that an animal could be cornered and perhaps injured there. The keeper saw the danger and the fence was changed.

Steel and concrete posts were taken out of a gorilla habitat to prevent the gorillas from using the posts like battering rams against glass walls. Clever primates delight in loosening bolts and screws and sometimes are able to take apart structures that are supposed to be monkey proof.

Zoo workers, from the director on down, have to be alert and observant or they may indeed have some unwelcome surprises.

A habitat for cows and chickens

The first time that someone suggested pigs and cows and sheep at a zoo, there must have been laughter. Imagine! A cow in a cage, a sheep baaing at visitors? Those are not exhibits for a zoological society. Or are they?

Many children, especially those from cities and suburbs, know more about foxes and penguins than about cattle, chickens, and pigs. When you think of this, then a farm setting at the zoo, where cows are milked, sheep sheared, and eggs gathered, is a good idea.

The big red barn at Lincoln Park Zoo is not surrounded by fields and pastures. Chicago streets, apartment houses, and a park are almost in its shadow.

The farm at the zoo gives a close-up view of how animals are raised, fed, and used on any large American farm.

Seeing the keepers at work in the farm buildings is a reminder of something else, too. It is important to clean and maintain exhibits. A crew of workers is kept busy cleaning, repainting, and rebuilding to keep the zoo a safe and healthy home for animals and an attractive place to visit.

Baby pigs are favorites with almost everyone who visits the Farm in the Zoo at Lincoln Park.

Is this an African waterhole being visited by hippopotamuses? It's the realistic habitat provided at the San Diego Wild Animal Park.

Moving out of the city

The San Diego Zoo is world famous. Its collection of mammals, birds, and reptiles numbers more than 5,000 and makes it the largest of any zoo.

A few years ago, planners for the San Diego Zoo decided to have a new and much different kind of animal environment. Outside the city, in a valley with foothills in the distance, the San Diego Wild Animal Park came into being.

Here zoo people duplicated natural living conditions for animals from Africa, Asia, Australia, and Central and South America. With thousands of acres available, it is possible to let animals roam and feed with almost as much freedom as they would have if they were in their own lands.

These animals are, in fact, freer of danger than they might ever be elsewhere. Predators—the animals which live by hunting and killing other animals for food—have separate living areas.

It's exciting to take the five-mile monorail ride and easy to forget that the animals you see are wild. There is also the aviary to visit, a Nairobi village, and an animal show where elephants lift logs and a red-tailed hawk dives from the sky for a bit of food held by its trainer.

The park entertains and educates its visitors. But there is more the park accomplishes because it specializes in breeding animals on the endangered species list. Several kinds of rhinoceroses, zebras, cheetahs, gazelles, and even the great North American golden eagle are among species which have been successfully bred there.

A large, well-trained staff of men and women, from research scientists to cafeteria helpers, work at the park. There are guides, animal trainers, musicians in the Nairobi village, and monorail operators, in addition to the curators, animal keepers, veterinarians, and other workers found in any large zoo.

Other wild animal parks, some public and some private, like Lion Country Safari, Inc. in California, are favorite places to visit. They're a creative way to exhibit animals and arouse curiosity about animal ways.

These lions lead healthier and longer lives at Lion Country than they might have in their natural habitat in Africa. Since they are predators, they are carefully separated from animals which would be their prey.

Petting an animal is what the Children's Zoo is all about. These domestic goats, some young and some adults, are patient and friendly.

Animals to pet and touch

Looking at animals is fine, but getting to know a hundred-year-old tortoise at close range or petting a baby goat can be an adventure, especially for youngsters.

At most large zoos a children's zoo is a separate, popular feature. Sometimes adults are only admitted if they are accompanied by children.

Girls and boys can pet and feed gentle animals and watch as a keeper cares for a baby such as a lion cub. Deer, baby goats, monkeys, rabbits, ducks, and once in a while a baby elephant, are fun to become acquainted with.

Keepers who are in the children's zoo must be ready to answer questions and help visitors remember that animals have feelings, too. All this is part of an important zoo goal: educating people to understand what animals are and can do.

Working at the Zoo

■ ■ ■

Managing a zoo is not like having a theater or a store or even a school. The animals are always there and cannot be neglected. Their lives depend upon the zoo staff.

Animals don't take holidays

Choosing and acquiring animals, making sure they are healthy and well housed, are zoo activities which require plenty of planning in advance.

There are other responsibilities, such as educating the public by making exhibits attractive and meaningful. But a zoo is not a museum. Birds, reptiles, and mammals are living creatures. When visitors leave, the zoo does not shut

The Bird House at Lincoln Park Zoo is a tropical setting for this macaw, being fed pieces of banana by keeper Dennis Pate.

Food is ready for delivery. Driver Everett Clawson looks back at fruit, grain products, vegetables, and meat prepared at the Lincoln Park Zoo commissary.

down. And what goes on around the clock is another part of the behind-the-scenes story.

What time is it?

The lions, tigers, leopards, jaguars, and cheetahs are pacing back and forth. Then the roars start. Loud as thunder, they echo through the building.

It is feeding time, and the animals know it.

The keeper appears. He is pushing a tray heaped with what look like huge hamburgers. Each weighs about ten pounds. He slides one into the lion's cage. Think how many hamburgers for a human being would be needed for one meal for the lion! Then think about the other animals hungrily waiting for the keeper to feed them.

The big cats need meat, and so do the polar bears, foxes, wolves, coyotes, hyenas, and others that in the wild either kill to feed themselves or eat what has been left by others.

But plenty of zoo inhabitants would die if they were only offered meat or fish. These are the ones which live on grain, nuts, leaves, fruit, grass, and other plant products.

To go grocery shopping for the zoo is quite a job because the shopping list includes practically everything imaginable that can be eaten: meat, fish, poultry, insects, grain, grass, fruit and vegetables.

The menu, or specific diet, for each species of animal is carefully planned by dietitians, veterinarians, and curators. There must be the proper amount and kind of food for good health. The needed vitamins and minerals have to be provided.

Unlike the hamburger you have for lunch, the "hamburger" fed to the big cats is made of ground horsemeat, beef, and chicken, with added vitamins and minerals.

For the antelopes, zebras, and many hoofed animals, specially processed grain foods are combined into a meal.

Fruits and vegetables are put together to make a giant "salad" for each of the great apes. Smaller salads feed the various kinds of monkeys.

Fish are prepared for birds like penguins and for sea lions and porpoises.

And then there is the full-grown elephant, who will probably eat 50 pounds of hay and 30 pounds of fruit and vegetables in a single day.

Some animals will not eat anything but live food. Crickets and other insects are therefore kept alive and fed to lizards and certain birds. Live mice, chickens, and other small animals are some-

These antelopes—impala and Thomson gazelles—and their bird guests are vegetarians. They are relatively inexpensive to feed.

times fed to snakes and alligators.

Each year a large zoo will need more than 50,000 pounds of meat, 20,000 pounds of fish, and tons of fruits, vegetables, and grain products. That's a lot of food to buy, and the grocery bill is big, too.

Zoos find it hard to feed all their animals when food costs rise. Some zoos ask people to "adopt" an animal by paying for its food for a year. There are many animals to choose from, some as small as mice and clams, others as large as ostriches and elephants. It can be a surprise to learn that it may cost more to feed a small animal with a special diet than another animal many times its size that eats food such as hay and grain.

In a recent year, Brookfield Zoo, near Chicago, had some of these animals for "adoption":

Freshwater clam, $5
African grass mouse, $10
Lion or giraffe, $800
Male gorilla, $1500
Elephants, from $1550 to $1750
Kodiak bear, $1600
White rhinoceros, $2000
Dolphin, $2200
Walrus, $8000

Food machinery is used in the Lincoln Park Zoo commissary, where many kinds of diets must be prepared every day. Roy Smith, a senior keeper, grinds celery.

You may wonder why a giraffe is so much cheaper to feed than a walrus. That's because the giraffe is fed hay and grain, while the walrus eats expensive and hard-to-get clams and fish.

Lincoln Park Zoo grows grass and other greens to feed some of its animals. There are no fields or meadows around the zoo, so how is the grass grown? It is grown without soil, in water which has all the needed plant foods added. This way of growing crops is called hydroponics. Using a method like this to provide grass for elephants is an unexpected kind of activity that goes on out of sight.

The kitchen at the zoo

The kitchen at a zoo is called a commissary. It is the place where food for all the animals is stored and prepared.

There are huge walk-in freezers and coolers, large storage bins, and shelves like those at a supermarket for canned goods.

In the commissary, workers cut up, grind, and weigh meat in portions for feeding. The prepared meat is put in buckets with colored bands. Keepers know which color identifies the food for the animals in their charge.

Fruits and vegetables are prepared in the commissary, too. Fish is processed, and grain products mixed together. Everything is measured and weighed and sent to its proper destination.

Growing grass in water-filled trays to which nutrients have been added is an unusual but successful way to feed some Lincoln Park Zoo animals.

Who does all the work?

Exactly the kind and amount of food fed each animal is the business of the dietitian. There must be a follow-up to make sure the diets are in fact what the animals will eat and thrive on.

Other workers who are involved in feeding include those who order food. This isn't always easy, for it can be a puzzle to know where to buy clams and crickets. But many foods are no problem

This monkey made a firsthand inspection of the operating lights in the infirmary at Lincoln Park Zoo.

because they are like those in the human diet.

The commissary workers are responsible for food preparation and delivery, often by truck, to every part of the zoo.

Sometimes it must seem as if all this is like keeping a motel or hotel with a lot of fussy guests, many with special menus. In one big way, a zoo is different. A balanced diet is always important, but animals have no need for variety from day to day.

Call the doctor!

It is just an average day at the zoo. Everything is fine, but—

The chimpanzee has a bad cold
The rhinoceros needs an eye operation
The zebra has a broken leg
An elephant has an infected toenail
The black leopard needs a tooth pulled
A peacock's bill should be trimmed
The Alaskan brown bear has stomach trouble
One great python has died

And these are only some of the problems the veterinarian and health care workers are likely to meet in their day-to-day, year-by-year work at the zoo.

Animals, like human beings, have their illnesses and their accidents. When they do, they have to see a doctor or go to the hospital.

The zoo doctors are doctors of veterinary medicine, and they are usually aided by special laboratory assistants. A veterinarian must complete a four-year course in animal medicine and be licensed, just as a medical doctor is.

The veterinarian treats animals as small as a mouse and as large as a moose, walrus, or elephant.

Veterinarians and animal specialists have learned much about protecting and caring for animals. Once life was short in the zoo for most animals. Today it is safe to say the zoo animals live longer and better lives than do many animals in their natural environment.

Now it is known that monkeys and apes easily pick up human diseases and infections. Glass walls protect these zoo residents from exposure to diseases caused by airborne organisms.

In the past, new animals often brought diseases and parasites with them and passed them on to the zoo population. Today this is prevented by putting each new animal in isolation to

Laboratory technician Joel Pond prepares a slide to examine through the microscope in the zoo infirmary. This kind of special equipment is valuable in maintaining animal health.

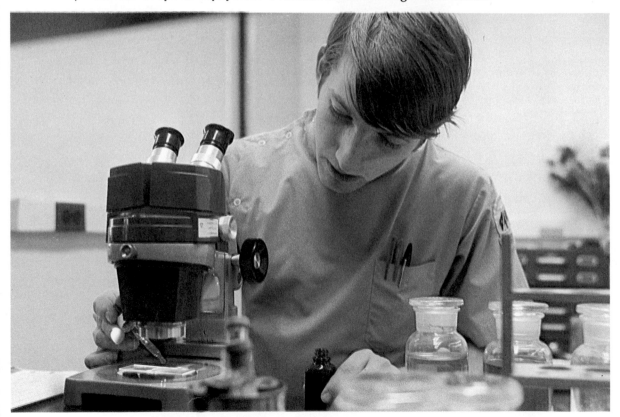

Look closely, and you'll see the baby jaguar, born at Lincoln Park Zoo, being given extra care. It is in an incubator like that used for newborn human babies who need special handling and protection from disease.

make sure it is free of parasites and disease before it enters its new home.

The zoo infirmary

The infirmary is headquarters for health care. In a big zoo it is an animal hospital with a place for examinations, a laboratory equipped with X-ray machines, microscopes, and testing equipment, and an operating room. Cribs very much like those used for premature human babies are ready for animal babies in need of special care.

Areas for isolating sick animals are also part of the infirmary. Of course it's not possible to accomodate a dolphin or a full-grown hippopotamus, but such problems are part of a zoo veterinarian's life.

Well-kept records are important. If an animal is sold or traded, it has a complete examination and its medical record is reviewed before the animal leaves the zoo for its new home.

When a bird, mammal, or reptile dies, the veterinarian does an autopsy to determine the cause of death. This information helps the staff learn what health problems may occur in other animals of the same species.

College and medical schools sometimes have access to the bodies of animals which have died, and thus future zoologists, biologists, and veterinary students have the chance to learn about animal structures and disease.

Be prepared

Cage bars and wide moats separate the animals from the outside world. They protect zoo visitors who might be careless or curious, or who forget that these are not tame pets.

The chance that an animal will escape and threaten anyone is remote. But the zoo staff is well prepared to handle the emergency if it comes. An alarm sounds, and employees respond quickly. Visitors are immediately directed to safety. The zoo, or a portion of it, is closed, and the zoo staff goes after the wanderer. Sometimes it's a matter of waiting until the escapee is hungry enough to return. At other times, keepers plan special strategies.

What about the wild animal parks, where lions go uncaged? The big cats may wander freely in their territory, but visitors are the ones who are confined. They must view from closed cars, a bus, or the monorail, depending upon the park.

At Lion Country Safari, in southern California, keepers in Jeeps have close contact with their charges and are alert for signs of trouble. They have rifles equipped to shoot tranquilizing darts. If tranquilizers will not calm the angry or upset beast, there are rifles with live ammunition.

The animals must have their safety protected, too. They can get into trouble on their own. Once an elephant slid down into a moat, fell, and was unable to get up. It was hoisted out by a crane. Another elephant was rescued from a similar mishap when it was led up a specially built earth ramp. Commissary

African lions may look as tame as house cats, but don't be fooled. The Lion Country Safari keeper in the jeep takes no risks with them.

Nets and cages are needed when animals must be moved or held for examination. Keeper Diane Penar shows nets of different sizes.

workers remember when a monkey escaped from the infirmary and raced through the kitchen. The lively patient threw food, pots, and pans at everyone chasing it.

The biggest threat to zoo animal health and safety, however, is from the public. The sign says

PLEASE DO NOT FEED THE
ANIMALS

but thoughtless people pay no attention,

and guards cannot always be present.

A zoo official explains, "Animals at the zoo are just like little children. Given their choice, most children would eat nothing but candy and ice cream, and forget nutritional foods they need. And if they did that, they'd eventually get sick. Well, the animals at the zoo are the same way. They much prefer peanuts and marshmallows and popcorn, but it's not good for them."

Special people with special skills

There are many kinds of zoos, large ones with thousands of animals, small ones with fewer than a hundred animals. Some have animals that represent only one specific geographic area, such as the forests of northern Wisconsin or the swamps of southern Florida.

Some zoos have traveling exhibits that go by truck to schools and parks. Some have special attractions such as shows featuring trained animal acts.

It is what goes on behind the scenes at any zoo which makes it work—work as a recreational spot to visit, a source of information, a place to learn about animals through observation, and a way to rescue endangered species.

A good zoo is not buildings and habitat exhibits, although these are necessary. It is not just animals. It is also the men and women who know and care about animals and want to share their knowledge and concern with others.

The zoo director, his assistant, the curators, the veterinarian, the commissary people, and the many keepers are some of the persons who work behind the scenes and have been introduced in this book.

There are other workers, too, the number and kind depending upon the size of the zoo and its budget. Some zoos have a curator for education and one for graphics—all the printed material, signs, and publications put out. A li-

Animals learn to trust their keepers, and keepers learn how far their charges can be trusted. The African elephant on the left and the Asiatic elephant on the right seem to be helping their keeper, John Lehnhard, at Lincoln Park Zoo.

There is plenty of office work to be done behind the scenes at any zoo, as executive secretary Alyce Fields well knows.

brarian who handles reference books and periodicals is valuable.

Night watchmen, guards (who at a city zoo may be policemen), leaders who conduct groups on tours, a secretary and other office workers—these are all important employees.

Volunteers at many zoos give their time and energy wherever they can help. Some are guides, some assist keepers.

To give you an idea of the number of zoo people, most of whom you may never see, here are some figures.

A zoo with more than 2,000 specimens belonging to about 390 species and subspecies requires a staff of 95 during summer months. It may have a director, an assistant director, five or six curators (including one each for mammals, birds, and reptiles), a full-time veterinarian, and a core of a dozen or so senior keepers backed up by some fifty other keepers. There is also an office staff, educational workers, and watchmen.

Is there a place for you behind the scenes at the zoo? If you're deeply interested in animals and their care, if you know how to handle them, there just might be. Whether you're a girl or boy, there are a few openings for young people, and especially for those who bring education as well as enthusiasm.

The small screech owl is being prepared by keeper David Kahn to travel to a Chicago school, where it will be exhibited. This is one of the educational projects of Lincoln Park Zoo.

Glossary

Glossary meanings given are for word usage in this book.

∎

a

artificial habitat, a man-made model of the place where an animal naturally lives.

autopsy, examination of a body after death, often to learn the cause of death.

aviary, a place, such as a building or enclosure, where birds are kept.

b

barrier, something that separates or confines. Fences, moats, and cage bars are zoo barriers.

biology, the science that deals with living things, both plants and animals.

bird sanctuary, a place of refuge or safety where birds are protected from their enemies.

breeding, mating to have young or offspring.

c

camouflage, an animal's color, stripes, or spots which help hide or conceal it.

class, in biology, a major grouping used to describe plants or animals which are alike in important ways. In the animal kingdom, a duck is an animal with a backbone which belongs to the class of birds.

commissary, a place where food is kept.

curator, a person in charge of a zoo or a part of a zoo, for example, the curator of birds.

d

dietitian, a person with special knowledge of the food needed for health and growth.

disease organism, a germ which causes disease.

e

endangered species, a species of animal which must be protected or it will die out.

environment, the area where an animal lives. A zoo environment is as much as possible like an animal's wild environment.

extinct, no longer living or existing.

g

gestation, the carrying of young in the mother's body before birth.

h

habitat, the place where a plant or animal is naturally found.

hydroponics, the growing of plants in water, to which necessary plant foods have been added.

i

infirmary, a zoo infirmary is where sick animals are treated.

inoculation, one means of disease prevention.

isolation, being kept apart or alone.

k

keeper, a person who takes care of animals.

m

mammal, an animal having a backbone, whose young is fed with milk, and whose body is more or less covered with hair.

moat, a trench, often filled with water, that acts as a barrier.

n

nocturnal, active at night. Bats are nocturnal animals.

p

parasite, an organism that lives on another organism. Fleas are parasites which live on dogs or cats.

physiology, a branch of biology which studies the bodies of living things and how they work.

population, the total number of individuals that make up a whole group. The zoo population is all the animals in a zoo.

predator, an animal that preys upon or eats other animals.

primate, the group of mammals which includes monkeys, apes, and lemurs.

q

quarantine, to isolate to prevent the spread of disease.

r

reptile, the class of animals which includes snakes, lizards, turtles, alligators, and crocodiles.

s

species, in plant or animal classification, a group which can interbreed with other animals of the same species. Dogs and wolves are two species of closely related animals who can mate and produce offspring.

stock, to provide with. The zoo is stocked with animals.

subspecies, in biology, a group of animals or plants that is very similar. Cinnamon bears and glacier bears are subspecies of American black bears.

survival, continuing to live. Fish need water for their survival.

t

territory, an area defended by an animal for hunting or breeding use.

tranquilizer, a drug used to calm an animal.

v

veterinarian, a person qualified by special education to treat animal diseases and injuries; a doctor of veterinary science.

z

zoologist, a student of zoology.

zoology, a branch of biology that deals with animals.